This book was purchased for the Didsbury Municipal Library through the generosity of the Knox United Thrift Store.

SIMPLY SCIENCE

Fossils

by Melissa Stewart

Content Adviser: Gina Wesley, Resident Graduate Student,
The Field Museum of Natural History, Chicago, Illinois

Science Adviser: Terrence E. Young Jr., M.Ed., M.L.S.,
Jefferson Parish (La.) Public Schools

Reading Adviser: Dr. Linda D. Labbo,
Department of Reading Education, College of Education,
The University of Georgia

COMPASS POINT BOOKS
Minneapolis, Minnesota

Compass Point Books
3109 West 50th Street, #115
Minneapolis, MN 55410

Visit Compass Point Books on the Internet at *www.compasspointbooks.com*
or e-mail your request to *custserv@compasspointbooks.com*

Photographs ©: Kevin Schafer/Corbis, cover; Philip James Corwin/Corbis, 4; Richard T.
Nowitz, 6; A.J. Copley/Visuals Unlimited, 7; Spencer Swanger/Tom Stack & Associates, 8;
Ken Lucas/Visuals Unlimited, 9; Larry Harwood, 10; Carolina Biological/Visuals Unlimited,
11; Charles & Josette Lenars/Corbis, 12; Brian Parker/Tom Stack & Associates, 13; Kent &
Donna Dannen, 14, 24; Lester V. Bergman/Corbis, 15 (all); Bruce Clendenning/Visuals
Unlimited, 16; Tom & Therisa Stack/Tom Stack & Associates, 18; Nathan Benn/Corbis, 19;
Jeff Daly/Visuals Unlimited, 20; Unicorn Stock Photos/Robert W. Ginn, 22; Jim Baron/
The Image Finders, 23; Unicorn Stock Photos/Dick Keen, 25; Unicorn Stock Photos/Chuck
Schmeiser, 27; Unicorn Stock Photos/Joel Dexter, 28.

Editors: E. Russell Primm, Emily J. Dolbear, and Catherine Neitge
Photo Researchers: Svetlana Zhurkina and Marcie Spence
Photo Selector: Linda S. Koutris
Designer/Page Production: Bradfordesign, Inc./Erin Scott, SARIN creative

Library of Congress Cataloging-in-Publication Data
Stewart, Melissa.
 Fossils / by Melissa Stewart.
  p. cm.— (Simply science)
Includes bibliographical references and index.
 ISBN 0-7565-0442-2 (hardcover)
 1. Fossils—Juvenile literature. I. Title. II. Simply science (Minneapolis, Minn.)
 QE714.5 .S74 2003
 560—dc21   2002010053

Table of Contents

*Note: In this book, words that are defined in the glossary are in **bold** the first time they appear in the text.*

When Reptiles Ruled

Millions of years ago, Earth was a very different place. Most of the land was warm and swampy. Reptiles ruled the land, the skies, and the sea.

Pterodactyls flew through the air. They dove into the water and caught fish with their sharp teeth. Seismosaurs were very tall. They spent their days eating the leaves and fruit from the tops of trees. Tyrannosaurs ate anything that crossed their path.

How do we know what Earth was like millions of years ago? Fossils tell us the story.

Dinosaurs that looked like this model walked on Earth millions of years ago.

Kinds of Fossils

Some fossils are the **remains** of plants, animals, and other living things. They show us what life was like millions of years ago. Paleontologists are scientists who look for and study fossils. Some paleontologists study the fossils of sharks' teeth. Other paleontologists work with the fossil bones of dinosaurs.

◀ These paleontologists have discovered some fossils.

Some dinosaurs had ▶ enormous skulls.

They have found that some dinosaurs
had skulls larger than your bed!

Trace fossils tell us how plants and animals lived millions of years ago. Eggs and nests are examples of trace fossils. Leaf **imprints** and burrows are too. Dinosaur footprints in hard rock are also trace fossils. The footprints can help paleontologists figure out how big an animal was. The footprints can also tell scientists how fast the dinosaur moved.

The homes of animals that lived millions of years ago are also trace fossils.

These dinosaur footprints are trace fossils.

A leaf imprint ▶

Paleontologists in Gallup, New Mexico, have found giant stone remains of termite nests. The nests show us how the ancient insects lived.

The remains of dinosaur nests can tell us how many eggs a dinosaur laid at one time. They can also help us understand how the parents cared for their young.

◀ The stone remains of an ancient termite nest in New Mexico

A coprolite ▶

Coprolites are fossils of animal droppings. Paleontologists study coprolites to learn where animals lived and what they ate. In the 1990s, a fossil hunter in Canada found a huge coprolite that may have been left behind by a *Tyrannosaurus rex*.

Where Fossils Form

Plants and animals die every day. Most do not become fossils. Most dead animals are eaten by other animals. Most dead plants rot. Over time they become part of the soil.

Many of the animal fossils that scientists have found formed from hard body parts. When the animals died, they were quickly buried by mud or sand.

A fossilized ammonite

The remains of most dead plants and animals become part of the soil.

Air could not reach them. Many fossils formed in rivers, sand dunes, and oceans. That is why the most common fossils are the remains of ocean animals.

Many fossils are formed from the hard body parts of underwater animals.

Casts of trilobite fossils found in California

Some of the easiest fossils to find are **trilobites**. No trilobites live on Earth today. Millions of years ago, however, they were common all over the world. These small ocean animals had oval bodies and a tough outer covering. They could walk on the seafloor or swim in shallow water.

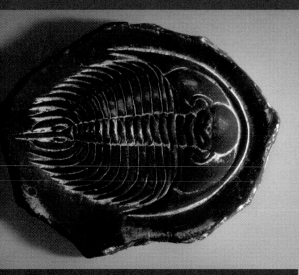

How Fossils Form

When a trilobite died, it sank to the muddy seafloor. Its soft body parts slowly rotted away. Sometimes its hard outer covering was left behind. As time passed, **minerals** in the ocean water took the place of the trilobite's hard covering. After thousands of years, the minerals hardened to form stone.

At the same time, layers of mud and sand piled up on top of the trilobite. The weight of the top layers pressed down on the lower layers.

◀ *Many layers of mud and sand built up to form the rock that trapped fossils.*

The mud and sand stuck together. Then they hardened to form rock. The trilobite fossil was trapped inside the newly formed rock.

Sometimes a fossil formed even when the trilobite's hard parts broke down. If layers of mud hardened around the outer covering before it disappeared, an imprint was left behind in the rock. This kind of fossil is called a **mold**.

When a trilobite died, its hard shell was sometimes left behind.

A fossil of a marine animal ▶

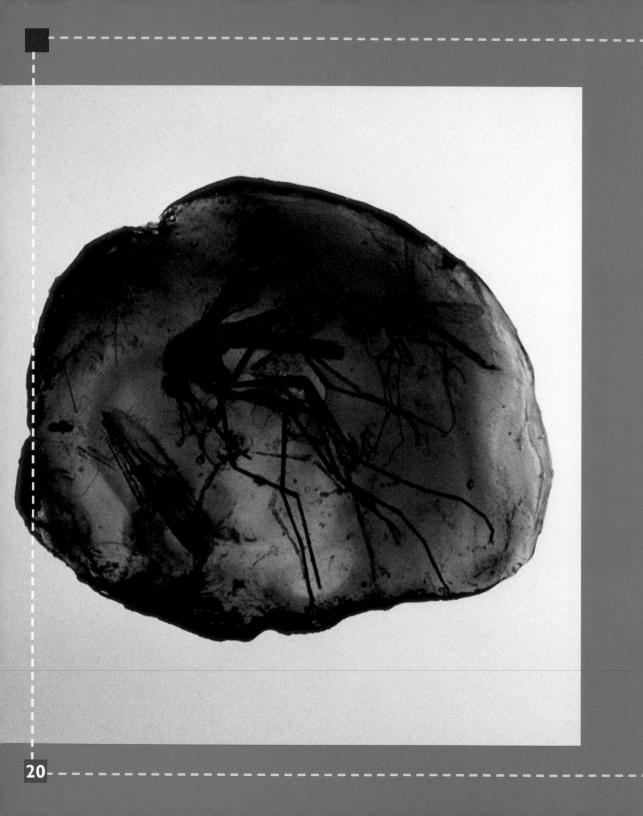

If a mold fills with minerals that harden to stone, a **cast** will form.

Most fossils form between layers of rock. They are also found in peat and tar. They may also be found in amber, which is hardened sap from trees that grew millions of years ago.

◀ *These insect fossils are trapped in amber.*

Finding Fossils

Many of the plants and animals that have lived on Earth are gone forever. Only a small number of living things become fossils. Still, there are many fossils to be found. They are more common than you might think.

The next time you go for a walk, look closely at the rocks.

It's fun to dig for fossils. ▶

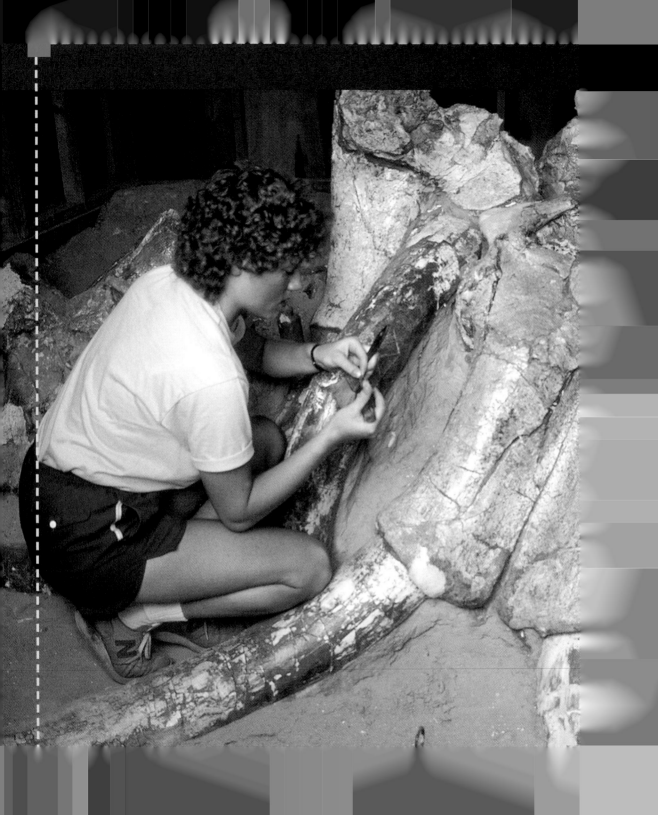

No matter where you live, there may be some fossils nearby. You might even be able to find some in your own backyard or at a local park. The next time you see a rock, pick it up and look at it closely. There might be a fossil inside.

You will probably not dig up the bones of a giant dinosaur, but you might find the fossils of some

◀ It takes many years of hard work to find huge fossils, like this mammoth skull.

You are much more likely to find small ▶ fossils, such as these sharks' teeth.

small sea animals. Some of the easiest fossils to find are sharks' teeth. Once you learn how to spot them, you can find them almost anywhere in the world.

To get started, call a local nature center or museum. Ask if they have any field trips for fossil hunters. Even if they do not, they may be able to suggest some good places where you can go to look for fossils. If you find a fossil, a fossil field guide can help you find out what it is. If you think you've found a really interesting fossil, you may want to get in touch with a paleontologist.

You and your family can have ▶
fun hunting for fossils.

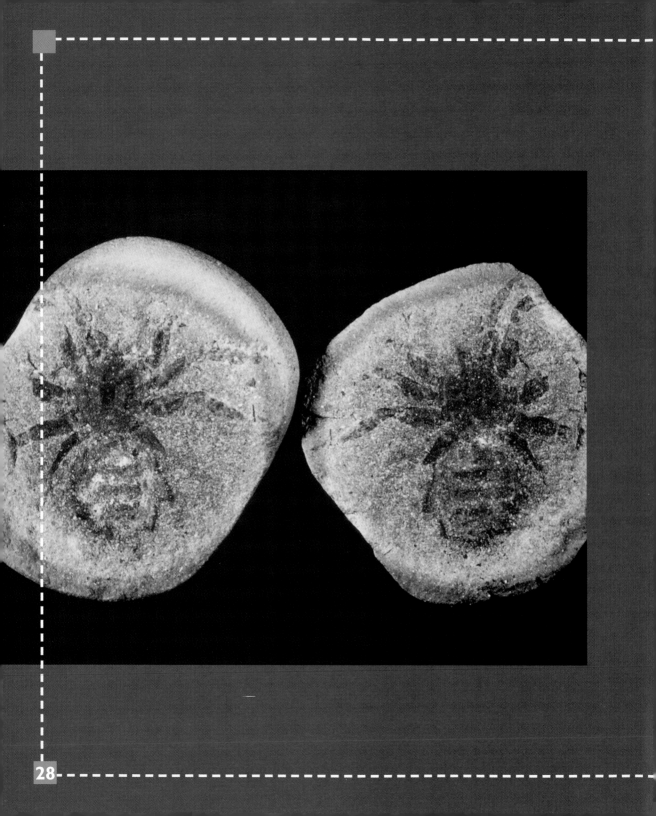

Perhaps a fossil you find will be put on display in a local museum. Maybe you will grow up to be a paleontologist yourself!

You might find something that's easy to identify, like these spider fossils.

Glossary

cast—a fossil that forms when sand, mud, or minerals harden inside a mold

imprints—marks made by pressing or stamping something on a surface

minerals—natural solid materials that are not alive; gold, salt, and copper are all minerals

mold—the imprint of an ancient creature in a rock

remains—parts of something that was once alive

trilobites—small sea animals that lived on Earth for about 300 million years and then died out

Did You Know?

• Earth is about 4.6 billion years old. Fossils show us that the first living things appeared about 3.5 billion years ago. The earliest animal fossils are about 600 million years old. The first humans lived about 120,000 years ago.

Want to Know More?

At the Library

Lessem, Don. *Dinosaurs to Dodos: An Encyclopedia of Extinct Animals*. New York: Scholastic, 1999.

Pellant, Chris. *The Best Book of Fossils, Rocks, and Minerals*. New York: Kingfisher, 2000.

Taylor, Paul D. *Eyewitness: Fossil*. New York: Dorling Kindersley, 2000.

On the Web

Dinosaur Eggs

http://www.nationalgeographic.com/dinoeggs/fintro.html

To find out how dinosaur eggs were found at three different sites and how they are being studied today

Petrified Forest National Park

http://www.desertusa.com/pet/du_pet_desc.html

To learn more about the beautiful fossils of logs at this park in Arizona

Through the Mail

U.S. Geological Society

USGS National Center

12201 Sunrise Valley Drive

Reston, VA 20192

For maps and advice about good places to hunt for fossils

On the Road

The Field Museum of Natural History

1400 S. Lake Shore Drive

Chicago, IL 60605

To visit a *Tyrannosaurus rex* skeleton named Sue

Index

About the Author

Melissa Stewart earned a bachelor's degree in biology from Union College and a master's degree in science and environmental journalism from New York University. She has written more than thirty books for children and has contributed articles to a variety of magazines for adults and children. In her free time, Melissa enjoys hiking and canoeing near her home in Marlborough, Massachusetts.